Bertie Wigg Amazing Ears

Dramatised from
David Cox and Erica James's story
by David Calcutt

Illustrated by Pat McCarthy

Oxford University Press

Oxford University Press, Great Clarendon Street, Oxford OX2 6DP

Oxford New York
Auckland Cape Town Dar es Salaam Hong Kong Karachi
Kuala Lumpur Madrid Melbourne Mexico City Nairobi
New Delhi Shanghai Taipei Toronto
With offices in
Argentina Austria Brazil Chile Czech Republic France Greece
Guatemala Hungary Italy Japan Poland Portugal Singapore
South Korea Switzerland Thailand Turkey Ukraine Vietnam

Oxford is a trade mark of Oxford University Press

© David Calcutt 1998

First published 1998

10 9 8 7 6 5 4 3

Adapted from the novel **Bertie Wiggins' Amazing Ears** by David Cox
and Erica James, published by Oxford University Press in 1995

ISBN-13: 978-0-19-918784-3
ISBN-10: 0-19-918784-3

Designed by Holbrook Design (Oxford) Limited

Printed in China

Cast list

There are twelve parts in this play, but you can act it out with a cast of six, if some actors take two parts and one actor takes three.

Bertie
Sadie / Royal Man / Prince Cecil
Mrs Lines / Royal Woman
Jimmy / The King
Mr Wiggins / Television Presenter
Mrs Wiggins / Princess Maud

There is also a non-speaking part for a camera operator at the beginning of Scene 3.

Scene 1

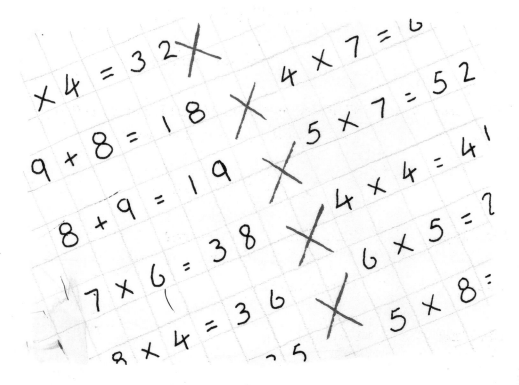

Bertie's classroom at school. There are three chairs. **Bertie** is sitting on one, **Sadie** on another, and **Jimmy** on another. **Bertie** is wearing a pair of very large ears. Their teacher, **Mrs Lines**, comes and stands in front of them. It is nearly the end of the school day.

Mrs Lines	Now, children. Just before you go home, we'll have a little tables test.

*The **children** groan.*

Mrs Lines	That's quite enough of that! It's only the fives. You all know your fives, don't you?

She speaks to Sadie.

Mrs Lines	Sadie. What is six times five?
Sadie	Thirty, Mrs Lines.
Mrs Lines	Very good.

She speaks to Jimmy.

Mrs Lines	Jimmy. What is three times five?
Jimmy	Fifteen, Mrs Lines.
Mrs Lines	Well done, Jimmy.

She speaks to Bertie.

Mrs Lines   Bertie. What is five times five?

Bertie   Five times five?

Mrs Lines   Yes, Bertie. That's what I said. What is five times five?

Bertie	Er…
Mrs Lines	Come on, Bertie Wiggins. Surely you know five times five.
Bertie	Five times five…
Mrs Lines	If you can't remember it, try and work it out.

Bertie	I'm trying to, Mrs Lines…

Jimmy calls out.

Jimmy	Look, Miss! His ears are waggling again!
Mrs Lines	Be quiet, Jimmy!
Jimmy	Wiggling and waggling! Look at them go!
Mrs Lines	Be quiet, I said! *(To Bertie)* Please do try and keep your ears still, Bertie. *(To Sadie)* Sadie. Do you know the answer to five times five?
Sadie	Yes, Miss. It's twenty-five.
Mrs Lines	That's right. *(To Bertie)* Bertie Wiggins, if you spent as much time on your work as you spend twitching your ears, you'd be as clever as Sadie. Perhaps even as clever as Prince Cecil!
Sadie	Bertie looks like Prince Cecil. Everybody says so.

Jimmy	There's only one difference. Prince Cecil hasn't got ears as big as Bertie's. Nobody has!
Mrs Lines	That's enough, Jimmy!
Jimmy	Sorry, Mrs Lines.

9

Mrs Lines   I hope you're all going to watch
Prince Cecil on television tonight.
The King's going to show everyone in the
country how clever his son is. He has such
clever children. Last year Princess Maud
played the trombone, and this year Prince
Cecil is going to say his tables.

Mrs Lines	*(To Bertie)* And you might learn a thing or two from him, Bertie.
Bertie	Yes, Mrs Lines.

Mrs Lines *looks at her watch.*

Mrs Lines	It's home time now. Off you all go. See you tomorrow.

Mrs Lines *goes. The three* **children** *stand up.*

Jimmy	I wish I had ears like yours, Bertie.
Bertie	Do you?
Jimmy	Yes. Because then I wouldn't have to walk all the way home. I'd just flap them and I could fly!

Jimmy *runs off, laughing.*

Sadie	Don't take any notice of him. I really like your ears. I think it's clever the way you make them wiggle.

Bertie	I don't make them wiggle.
	They do it on their own.
Sadie	That's even better.
	You should go on television with them.
	You'd be famous.
Bertie	I don't want to be famous,
	and I don't want to go on television.
	All I want is to be able to do my tables!
Sadie	Perhaps you will, one day.
	I'd better go home, now.
	I don't want to miss seeing Prince Cecil.
	Goodbye, Bertie. See you tomorrow.
Bertie	Bye, Sadie.

*Sadie goes. **Bertie** goes, looking very
fed up, in another direction.*

Scene 2

For the next scene, the stage is split in two. Half of it is Bertie Wiggins' home. The other half is the street outside the house.

It is the same evening, at Bertie's home. **Mr** *and* **Mrs Wiggins** *enter. They are getting ready to watch television.* **Mr Wiggins** *mimes turning on the television set.*

Mr Wiggins   *(Calls)* Bertie! Hurry up!

Mrs Wiggins   *(Calls)* It's almost time for the television!

Mr Wiggins   *(Calls)* It's almost time for the King to make his speech!

Mrs Wiggins   *(Calls)* And for Prince Cecil to show how clever he is.

Mr Wiggins   *(Calls)* Come on, Bertie. You'll miss it.

Mr Wiggins *speaks to Mrs Wiggins.*

Mr Wiggins   What is the matter with him this evening?

Mrs Wiggins	I don't know.
Mr Wiggins	He's been fed up ever since he came in from school.
Mrs Wiggins	Perhaps he's had a bad day.

Bertie enters, still looking fed up.

Mr Wiggins	There you are! What's the matter? Don't you want to watch Prince Cecil on television?

Bertie	No.
Mrs Wiggins	No? Why not? I thought you liked Prince Cecil. You know how much you look like him.
Bertie	He hasn't got ears like mine, though, has he?
Mr Wiggins	No, and you'll never be on television like him if you keep on flapping them.
Bertie	I'm going outside.
	Bertie walks away from Mr and Mrs Wiggins, to the other half of the stage. He sits down outside the house with his chin in his hands.
	Inside the house Mrs Wiggins speaks to Mr Wiggins.
Mrs Wiggins	I think you said the wrong thing there, dear.

Mr Wiggins	Well, he shouldn't keep on flapping them like that. Let him sulk. It's time for the King.
	Mr and Mrs Wiggins sit down to watch television. Outside, a man and a woman enter, see Bertie, and stop.
Royal woman	Goodness me! I don't believe it! It's amazing!
	They step closer to Bertie and look very hard at his face. Bertie stares back at them, puzzled.
Royal man	It truly is amazing!
Bertie	What is?
Royal woman	You! *(To royal man)* I've never seen anything like it in my life!
Bertie	I hope you don't mean my ears.
Royal woman	*(To Bertie)* I don't mean your ears. I mean your face! It's just like him! Are your parents in?

Bertie   Yes. They're in there.

Royal man   Good. We must talk to them straight away.

> *The **man** mimes knocking on the door.
> **Mr** and **Mrs Wiggins** get up and go
> to answer it. They mime opening the
> door.*

Royal woman   Hello. We're from the Royal Palace. How do you do?

> *She holds out her hand. **Mr** and **Mrs**
> **Wiggins** are completely surprised.*

Mr Wiggins   Oh…! How do you do…?

> *He shakes her hand.*

Mrs Wiggins   The Royal Palace…!

> *She shakes the royal woman's hand.*

Royal man   Yes. Pleased to meet you.

He holds out his hand.
Mr Wiggins *shakes it.*

Mr Wiggins   We're pleased to meet you.

Mrs Wiggins *shakes*
the royal man's hand.

Mrs Wiggins	Very, very pleased indeed!
Royal man	Your son must come with us straight away to the television studio.
Mrs Wiggins	Our Bertie?
Mr Wiggins	Go with you?
Mrs Wiggins	What for?
Mr Wiggins	What's he done?
Royal woman	It isn't what he's done. It's what he's going to do. It's what he is!
Mrs Wiggins	What do you mean?
Royal woman	He's Prince Cecil!
Mr Wiggins	No, he's not! He's our Bertie. Bertie Wiggins.
Royal man	I mean he looks like Prince Cecil. Look at this photo.

*The **man** shows a photo to Mrs Wiggins. Meanwhile, the **woman** puts a crown on Bertie's head.*

Royal woman   Just like Prince Cecil!

Royal man   And that's why we need him. Prince Cecil has red spots. It could be chicken pox. He can't go on television tonight. But everyone will be watching. We can't disappoint them. So, the King has ordered a secret search for a Prince Cecil look-alike. And we've found him!

Mr Wiggins	You mean our Bertie's got to go on television?
Mrs Wiggins	And pretend to be Prince Cecil?
Royal man	Yes.
Mr Wiggins	We'll be famous!
Royal woman	No, you won't. No one must ever know. When Bertie goes on television, everyone must think he is the Prince. It's a secret you must all keep forever.
Mrs Wiggins	Will we meet the King and Queen?
Royal man	Yes.
Mr Wiggins	Will there be a reward?

Royal woman	Perhaps. Now, please. We must hurry. We must drive straight to the television studios.
Bertie	Wait a minute –
Royal woman	There isn't time.
Bertie	I can't pretend to be Prince Cecil!
Royal man	What do you mean?

Mrs Wiggins	Of course you can, Bertie, dear.
Mr Wiggins	It's your duty, and you'll do as you're told!
Bertie	But I can't. As soon as people see me on television they'll know I'm not him.
Royal woman	I understand. It's your ears you're worried about. Yes, they are rather large. But I thought perhaps we could stick them down with sellotape –
Bertie	It's not my ears. It's my tables.
Mrs Wiggins	Your tables?
Bertie	Prince Cecil's going on television to show how clever he is. He's supposed to say his tables. I can't. I don't know mine.
Royal man	Is that all? Silly boy! You don't have to be clever. All the answers will be on a screen in front of you. You can read, can't you?
Bertie	Of course I can!

Royal man	Good. No one else will be able to see the screen. And no one will know that you can't do your tables.
Bertie	Oh. I see.
Royal woman	Now, really, we must get along. It's almost time for the programme to start.

> *The **woman** takes the crown off Bertie's head. She looks at his ears and shakes her head.*

Royal woman	And we must do something about those ears!

> *The **woman**, the **man**, **Bertie**, and **Mrs** and **Mr Wiggins** all go.*

Scene 3

The television studios. A **camera operator** brings on a chair, and a camera, and points the camera at the chair.

The **King** enters, wearing one crown and carrying another. He paces up and down, very worried.

King

I can't wait much longer. They must have found someone who looks like Prince Cecil by now. I will not wait any longer! This is terrible! This is awful! This is dreadful!

*The **woman** enters with **Bertie.***

Royal woman

This is Bertie Wiggins.

King	Goodness me! He looks just like the Prince. Apart from his ears. Here. Hide them with this crown.

*The **King** puts a crown on Bertie's head, over his ears.*

King	There. That's better. Now no one will be able to tell the difference.
Bertie	But Your Majesty, I'm not Prince Cecil –
King	I know. You couldn't be with those ears.
Bertie	And I don't want to pretend to be him –
King	What!
Royal woman	Silly boy. Of course you do. *(To the King)* He's just joking, Your Majesty.
King	Not a very funny joke, if you ask me. Now, just go and sit down over there and do as you're told. It's just about time for the television programme to start. I'll be waiting over here. And I'll be watching you.

*The **King** goes over to one side and watches. The **woman** takes Bertie to the chair and sits him down.*

Royal woman   Here you are. Now, do you see the camera?

Bertie   Yes.

Royal woman   And do you see that screen
next to the camera?

Bertie   Yes.

Royal woman   The answers to all the sums will appear on
that screen. All you have to do is read them
every time you're asked a question. Nobody
else can see the screen, so it will look like you
know the answers.

Bertie   That's cheating.

Royal woman   Do you want to sit there
and not know the answers?

Bertie	I don't want to sit here at all.

*The **King** calls across.*

King	Is everything all right? He's not being awkward, is he?

*The **woman** calls back to the King.*

Royal woman	No, Your Majesty. Everything's fine. He's ready now.

*The **woman** walks over to one side, to stand next to the King.*

King	Good. Just in time too. The programme's starting now.

*The **television presenter** enters, stands next to Bertie, and speaks to the camera.*

Presenter	Good evening, everyone. Tonight we are happy to welcome our young prince to the show. If you remember, last year his sister, Princess Maud, played the trombone. And wasn't she clever. Now, this year, Prince Cecil is going to show how clever he is by saying his eight times table.

He speaks to Bertie.

Presenter	That's right, isn't it, Prince Cecil?

Bertie nods.

Presenter	Good. Now. Here's the first question. One times eight.
Bertie	One times eight is eight.
Presenter	Two times eight.
Bertie	Two times eight is sixteen.
Presenter	Very good so far. Three times eight.
Bertie	Three times eight is…

Bertie looks at the screen. A frightened look comes on his face. He stops.

Presenter	Yes?
King	What's the matter? Why doesn't he answer?
Royal woman	The screen's gone blank. It's broken down. The answer isn't there!

Presenter	Well, Prince Cecil? What is three times eight?
Bertie	Three times eight... er...
King	What are we going to do?
Royal woman	I don't know.

King   He's making my son look like a fool!

Presenter   Are you all right, Prince Cecil?

Bertie   No. I don't feel very well. I'm hot. My ears have gone all twitchy. I must take my crown off.

He takes off the crown.

King	He's taken off the crown! Everyone can see those ears of his!

Bertie takes off his shoes.

King	Now what is he doing? He's taking his shoes off!

Bertie takes his socks off.

Royal woman	And his socks, Your Majesty.

King	His socks! What on earth does he want to take his socks off for?

Bertie starts counting on his fingers and toes, trying to work out the answer.

King	What's he doing with his toes?

Royal woman	He seems to be… counting them!

King	Counting them! Why does he want to count his fingers and toes? Doesn't he know how many he's got?

Royal woman   I think he's trying to work out
the answer to the sum.

King   Oh, no! This is terrible! I can't look.

*The **King** hides his face in his hands.*

Royal woman   I think you had better look, Your Majesty.

King   Why?

Royal woman   The boy's ears – they're starting to waggle!

King   What!

                      *He takes his hands from his face and
                      looks.*

Presenter   Prince Cecil, do you know
                      your ears are waggling?

Bertie   Yes. And there's nothing I can do about it.

Presenter   *(To the camera)* Ladies and gentlemen, this is
                      amazing. I've never seen anything like this before!
                      Prince Cecil's ears are waggling on television. You
                      can actually see them. There they are, going
                      backwards and forwards.

King   This is a disaster! We must put a stop to it!
                      I'm going to stop the programme straight away!

                      *The **King** is just about to walk across
                      to Bertie and the presenter, when the
                      woman calls out.*

Royal woman Twenty-four! They've waggled twenty-four times.
And that's the answer to the sum.
Three times eight is twenty-four!

Bertie My ears knew the answer!

Presenter Twenty-four! His ears have answered the
question! Let's just see if it works again.
What is four times eight?

Bertie   Four times eight. Let me see…

Presenter   They're waggling again. Let's count.
One, two, three, four…

*The **presenter** carries on counting
silently while the **King** and the
woman speak.*

Royal woman   Did you see that, Your Majesty? The boy's ears
came up with the answer to the question.

King	Yes. Perhaps things aren't going to be such a disaster after all.
Royal woman	That boy certainly has amazing ears.
Bertie	Thirty-two! My ears waggled thirty-two times!
Presenter	And that's the answer to the question! Four times eight is thirty-two. So, that's how you do it!
Bertie	Yes. And all this time I never knew.

*The **King** walks in front of the camera.*

King	Ladies and Gentlemen, as you can see, my son, Prince Cecil, has the most amazing talent –
Presenter	And ears –
King	And just to prove how clever he is, I will now ask him to do some really hard sums –

*Suddenly, **Princess Maud** and
Prince Cecil come running on.
Prince Cecil has red spots on his
face.*

Maud   Stop it, Dad!

King   Princess Maud! Prince Cecil!
                What are you doing here?

Maud	We've come to tell everyone the truth. (*She points at Bertie*) That is not the real Prince Cecil!
King	(*Angrily*) What are you talking about, Maud?
Cecil	I'm the real Prince Cecil.
Presenter	But if you're Prince Cecil, who's this?
Bertie	I'm Bertie Wiggins!
King	Stop the show! Turn the cameras off!
Maud	No! Leave them on! We want everyone to know the truth!
King	Shut up! Prince Cecil! You're ill! You should be at home in bed!
Cecil	I'm not really ill. Maud painted these spots on my face.
King	(*To Maud*) You!

Maud   And I can't really play the trombone. Last year
             I had to pretend I could, and it was horrible!

Cecil   And I didn't want to go on television because
             I can't really do sums.

             *The **woman** joins them.*

Royal woman   It's true. Everything has just been pretend.
                    The King ordered me to go and find someone
                    who looked like Prince Cecil to take his place.

Cecil   And when we saw him on television,
                    we knew we had to stop the show.

Maud   Because we hate it. It makes everyone laugh at us.
                    They think we're too good to be true.

King	But we have always gone on the Royal Television Show! That's what it's for. To show how clever you are.
Cecil	But we're not! We're not really clever.
Maud	*(Pointing at Bertie)* The only really clever one is him.
Royal woman	His ears are, anyway.
King	What's going to happen to us now?

Presenter   And what's going to happen to my show?

Bertie   I've got an idea.

*Everybody turns to look
at Bertie.*

Bertie   Why don't you put on a show that children will
really like?
Children from all over the country
can go on it.

Maud   You mean a talent-spotting show?

Bertie   That's right.

Royal woman   What a good idea!

Cecil   It's a great idea!

Presenter   Just the kind of show lots of people
will want to watch.

*The **King** is frowning.*

Maud	Go on, Dad. Say yes.
Royal woman	The Royal Talent-Spotting Show. I think you should agree, Your Majesty.
King	Very well. But my children must be the stars –
Cecil	No, Dad, we won't.
Maud	We never want to show off again.

Royal woman	They're right, Your Majesty. There's only one person who can be the star of the show.
King	Who?
Royal woman	Bertie Wiggins, and his amazing waggling ears!

The End

Treetops Playscripts
Titles in the series include:

Stage 10
The Masked Cleaning Ladies of Om
by John Coldwell; adapted
by David Calcutt
    single: 0 19 918780 0
    pack of 6: 0 19 918781 9

Stupid Trousers
by Susan Gates; adapted by David Calcutt
    single: 0 19 918782 7
    pack of 6: 0 19 918783 5

Stage 11
Bertha's Secret Battle
by John Coldwell; adapted
by David Calcutt
    single: 0 19 918786 X
    pack of 6: 0 19 918787 8

Bertie Wiggins' Amazing Ears
by David Cox and Erica James; adapted
by David Calcutt
    single: 0 19 918784 3
    pack of 6: 0 19 918785 1

Stage 12
The Lie Detector
by Susan Gates; adapted by David Calcutt
    single: 0 19 918788 6
    pack of 6: 0 19 918789 4

Blue Shoes
by Angela Bull; adapted by David Calcutt
    single: 0 19 918790 8
    pack of 6: 0 19 918791 6

Stage 13
The Personality Potion
by Alan MacDonald; adapted
by David Calcutt
    single: 0 19 918792 4
    pack of 6: 0 19 918793 2

Spooky!
by Michaela Morgan; adapted
by David Calcutt
    single: 0 19 918794 0
    pack of 6: 0 19 918795 9

Stage 14
Petey
by Paul Shipton; adapted
by David Calcutt
    single: 0 19 918796 7
    pack of 6: 0 19 918797 5

Climbing in the Dark
adapted from his own novel
by Nick Warburton
    single: 0 19 918798 3
    pack of 6: 0 19 918799 1